THE WINGBACK CHAIR

Joan Colby

FUTURECYCLE PRESS

www.futurecycle.org

Published by FutureCycle Press
Lexington, Kentucky, USA

ISBN 978-1-938853-59-3

In memory of my mother,
Grace Turbyfill

CONTENTS

THE WINGBACK CHAIR

I picture her sitting
In the wingback chair
Before the window framed with the pendulous
Branches of the stricken ash.

A small glass of ginger ale
On the side table, her tissues,
The soft gardening gloves to keep her
From scratching her face,
Skin so delicate, each bruise
An archipelago of age.

It is the middle of things she can't see,
The blur where faces used to be.
She misunderstands the television
Confiding to her best ear.

Marlene Dietrich died at 90
In her parents' apartment. How good
They could be with her.

Later, the news: Paris apartment, easy
To rationalize how she got it wrong,
Harder to accept how she failed to question.

She pulls her hair out strand by strand
As if about to weave a tale
Like those she once told me:
Mari Ruadh who wielded a horsehair
To build an impenetrable barrier
As she fled a father's vengeance
With her true love.

These barriers: I ask about the talking book
She listened to last night. "Informational,"
She says, wincing from my interrogations.

I know it's the short-term
Memory bank that is robbed hourly,
How old-style safes are safer;
But the bullion of her lost mother, father,
Sisters, brothers, husband makes her cry.

Every day, I reassess the advantages
Of great age. How people wish to
Live a hundred years. What are they
Thinking? "If I retained my faculties,"
They say, not knowing
That makes it worse.

I could chop these images
Into sparkling shards,
But the way she diminished
Was slow and easy,

A repetitive gesture like a salute
To all the angels attending
Her departure.

The neurologist explains deterioration
Of the frontal lobe, but I don't know.
I don't know what she is seeing
With the blind eye of attrition.

The chair's plush wings
rise behind her.

What Is Saved

Preserved and boxed, the gown
Is made to lie in wait,
Satins and laces intact
For a future bride.

Of the tiered cake,
A giant slice
In the freezer specially wrapped,
White on white.
Some anniversary hence
They'll find it tasteless.

The shrunken bride and groom
Who perched upon its frosting
Are now blank faces staring
At black on black
In a box within a closet.

The album, once admired,
Must ride the heavy gloss
Of a day so pertinent
Its artifacts must not be lost
Even if love is.

The Wyoming Pagoda

The smell of the sage
Is what reminds her,
Stepping out of the Prius,
But first she looks away
At the mountains bent like
Burdened women frozen
In their footsteps. The grey
Flank of cloud. A foothill rising.
So finally she must behold
What's left: The collapsing pagoda
Like a stack of parasols.
It would be beautiful, he said.
A permanence. A home.

She'd imagined friends drinking
Saki or Mexican beer. An appaloosa
In the corral. The sun coming up
Out of the badlands. She was just
A child when he fell
From the parapet, leaving it all
Unfinished, a crazy ruin
Where tourists speculate on hubris,
How tower builders meet
The fate of confusion,
A babble of tongues, or a misstep.

She doesn't believe the rumors–
Ghost-cries of buzzards,
Specters of sheep that vanish
Before one's eyes or the stallion
That races the horizon at moonrise,

How it was the war or drugs,
A maze he walked drawing
Blueprints in his mind
As the breath of the Chinook
Warmed him to the task.

Cheap talk. What she remembers
Is how, when he recognized
What was ordained, he tried.

CHAINS

Gold paper chains for festivals.
Chains of flowers a child weaves.
Chains of promises given by lovers.
Ball and chain of matrimony.
Invisible chains of chromosomes.

Blacksmiths say a chain
Is the hardest thing to forge.

Chains brutal and immense to
Keep shuffling men in line,
Picks on shoulders, singing
While a guard with a shotgun hawks tobacco juice.

A white-faced woman manacled
On the cover of a cheap magazine. The lethal chain
A rattler shakes. The way music rises
Link by link. How one word curves
Around another and locks on sense.

MIXED MARRIAGE

A woman living in the house behind the slag pile
Giving her paycheck to her parents.
A man freezing everything in the lens of his Rolleiflex,
Sepia visions.

It was destined they would meet.
That he would ride the El through decrepit neighborhoods
For a supper of Irish stew in her mother's kitchen.
His room at the northside Y, a square of loneliness
Pitched perfectly around his presence,
And she, sleeping upstairs in a converted attic,
Counting the black beads, the mysteries.

It was a mixed marriage. The priest
Barred them from the sanctuary.
A cross burned between their hearts.
They could never tell
Each other their needs.

Her mind wimpled like a nun's skull.
His eyes drilled into books.
I was born into their house.
Their fingers spread with loss,
Touching this new thing,
Not his, not hers,
Not the interpreter
They'd hoped for.

FRANKENSTEIN

Enter the world with your improbable sutures and blockhead.
You were conceived in spectral moonlight,
A devastation of evolution.

Her idea sprang from a bet,
Something casual as
Putting on a slipper.

Confess, you were not up to what
She envisioned, a miracle
Of innocence without sin,

No legs entwined to beget you.
In that age, science was just
Assuming its white coat

And speculum. Yet she chose
A drafty castle for the set,
Miasma of steam and shock,

All sorts of special effects
To prompt Bethlehem back into its book
Of simplicity. You were no good–

That large hulking stride,
How people turned away, even the child
At first, frightened– but then

Compassion opened its petals.
You were struck dumb, a prickling
In your cadaver coat.

Watching her float,
What did you feel, if anything?
Your author forecast a journey;

The latitudes of fear
Costumed your foolish career.
Her intention was serious:

A parable like those that made
Jesus famous. Yet there was always
Something dubious, something deflated

Like the prayer of an atheist.
She blamed it on the moon
That night in Cologny.

Confusing her dreams,
The names too became confused
In all the resurrected Halloweens,

Master and monster united
In one garbled body
Lurching door to door.

GARGOYLES

The sculptor tells us that he prefers grotesqueries.
A quirky riff or maybe just nostalgia for an age
Where saints and dragons mixed it up.

Romanus, Bishop of Rouen, raised his crucifix
To transfix the fire-breathing Gargouille,
Its bat wings spread in defiance.

Torched at the stake, its hot head
Refused to catch. Nailed up on bulwarks
To spew rainwater. Wasserspeier.
Grotesque gullet. Architectural device.

Others merely ornamental, like these.
Creatures from the Garden of Earthly Delights.
Monster infants with cherub wings,
Clawed toes and wrinkled hands,
Trident tails, little perky horns.

They can be purchased.
The sculptor takes orders.
I like the vengeful ones,
Vampire visages
And Lucifer wings.

RED RIDING HOOD

The age of innocence ends at seven.

First of all, the grandmother
With her ancient demands. The insistence
Of the aged to be honored. The woods
Were heavy with snow. All the trees
Bent over. If this was submission,
It was involuntary.

There must have been a mother who provided
What was to be offered. Who was torn
Between generations, their common enemy.
How she tried to appease them: the old woman
In her bed, the child ruddy with pleasure.

Everyone must have known what lurked
In the boundless places, sly and conniving.

Let us remember the child, too, was complicit.
Heedless, eager to go where she would not
Be commanded. Her red cloak in the forest.
Her basket of sweetness.

MEDITATION OF THE WITCH

They battened on my roof, those two.
She, with her corkscrew curls and
Little serpent smile.
He, a rough-thatched yokel
With a stupid fixed stare.

What gobblers they were. I remember
How they'd rip hunks of chocolate
From the beams and cram jagged panes
Of spun-sugar in greedy mouths.

Nighttime, I'd tell them
How the moon lost her daughter,
How the wind earned its wings.
Nothing interested them
But eating.
She devoured the curtains;
He started in on the floorboards.

I took to her
Despite myself, but that bullock-eyed lad
With his shaggy stubborn sulk–
The devil couldn't reason with such a dullard.
"Fetch water," I told him. He sat in bed,
Munching the sheets, getting
Fatter and fatter.

Later it was said I jailed him
To plump him up. That's a laugh.
If I did fry a boy,
It would be a toothsome one,
Not that lardy Hansel.

She tried to kill me, you know.
Oh, everyone said it must have been
An accident, but it wasn't.
I thought *water, water*
And the stove went out. She
Was at the well drawing up the bucket,
Cool as you please. He was in the stable
Demanding *more more.*

That night I dreamed their father
Found a sack of diamonds.
They swallowed it, of course.

At the gate, she turned–
I supposed as a goodbye–
Eating one of those apples
I told her never to touch.

I think of her sometimes,
Of both of them.
Hungry as hogs. Hungry for any damn thing.
Wanting to swallow the road
Home, the landscape of time.
Always dropping crumbs the birds seize
And then asking
"Which way did we come?"

A FELLA MAYBE

Examining our new stock trailer, Ralph says,
"A fella could maybe take this hitch"– his hand
Rubs the one on our old truck– "and move it
Up a snitch, weld it back on."

A fella could maybe do that. It's always a fella,
Never him or you or me.

I'd like to meet that fella
Who can maybe fix the well pump,
Clean out the clogged catch basin, roof the
Barn in one day's labor, snare the raccoons
That raid the grain room, refinish
The old oak floors, plant a meadow
Of purple flowers, sing like a troubadour,
Take me to Rome on a vacation,
Show me where the wild things are,
And maybe even dance.

KAREN'S QUILT SHOP

BY CHANCE OR BY APPOINTMENT
Says the sign for Karen's Quilt Shop
Spray-painted on the bricks
Of the Wasco post office.

I prefer by chance,
Perhaps one day strolling
With no purpose and, egad,
Here's Karen's Quilt Shop!

And though I have no talent
For needles, I might go in,
Look over the fabrics, the skeins
Of colored yarns, the frames
To hold the work tight,
The batting that keeps a sleeper warm,

The threads that can whip a life
In neat star shapes or maybe
The crazy kind.

THE PIANO STUDENT

The first year I practice on a mock keyboard
Like a mute singing.
My parents want to be sure I am serious.
They think music
Is in the fingers or the eye.
My mother jokes of her tin ear.

A piano is an immense richness,
Ebony and ivory
Felts with their plush pounce,
The soft pedal like a cat's paw.

I sit for hours before it
Examining grace notes, trills,
Staccatos, the whole notes full
As Grade A eggs, the base
Clef a huge comma.

I love flats, the laid-back
Romance of them. My fingers seek
Them of their own volition.

But sharps, how they torment me:
Skinny women with the tense
Metal voices of mothers.
I can feel their brass in my mouth
Like a curb bit. It is hard
For me to play in such a key.

Outside the lace-veiled windows,
The streets are full of action.
I sit at the piano inviolate.

Arpeggio, andante– I blur
In their spell, commandeered.

Each Saturday, I go to the convent
To be subjected to Czerny.
My stubby fingers, inherently unfit,
Stumble through the intricate runs,
Outdo themselves and dance.
The metronome pounds out tempos
Like God. Sister sits
At my side, black and white
As the keys
We unlock. I feel religious
About Mozart, Chopin, Bach.

When I went under ether,
Quarter notes danced in my eyes
Around an intense bonfire.
The treble clef swung its cat tail
Until I was unconscious,
My head one giant recital
Flowing down through my fingers
Into these notes:
A, the mother, anxious and careful;
F, the father, preoccupied, always leaning
Like an umbrella into the wind;
G, the best friend who walks
Me halfway home and I walk
Her back;
And myself, middle C,
The axis, the first note
I ever heard.

ON ANGELS

I never cared much for angels,
Having been forced, in the first grade,
To share my desk with one.
We were never
Introduced, although I was assured
He had guarded me since birth. There is
No etiquette for dealing with angels.
They come at inopportune
Moments with announcements
That change lives– lives that were probably
Perfectly content to begin with.

Angels are grandstanders,
Bombastic politicians. They say
"Hark" and "Be Not Afraid,"
"Go Into the Desert." Then they
Fly off.

Remember, also, there are dark ones,
Rebels who roller-coasted down
The Milky Way– wild hellions.
Their swan wings changed to bats';
Their haloes peaked into horns.
Ah, they snuck into our heads
At mass with black satchels
Of impure thoughts. The one named Sloth made us
Look out the window during math.
The one named Disrespect made us mock
The nuns in their black caves.
Like angels, nuns had no bodies,
Only faces, hands, black shoes,

Beads that clicked as they walked
In a sort of spiritual heartbeat.
Like angels, they were one
With mysteries. They spoke
Of faith and grace ungraspable
As angels.
Sister Philomena told us
Of a terrible offense,
Pagans pissing on the host,
Desecrating the Eucharist.
We gasped
As if angels were flying down our throats.
What was famine or war
Compared to this?
The way to deal with pagans
Was to buy their babies. I owned two
On the chart of the Propagation
Of the Faith. One brown. One yellow.
My quarters would buy them angels
Of their own.
    Only Catholics had angels.
They seemed to be useless as pet rocks,
But in fact they were watching
Over you. I named mine Golden Wings.
When the car carrying Thomas Duffy and his entire
Family was crushed by the Illinois Central,
I knew their angels must have been daydreaming.
The wicked angel of daydream sat at my elbow.

Sister gave me a holy card.
On it an angel proclaimed
To demure Mary
That she was growing fat

With the seed of god.
A border of baby angels
Grinned. Fluffy clouds were
Stuck in the blue sky of Jerusalem.
A visit from angels
Is always portentous.
They leave a wake
of holy bastards and pillars of salt.
They blow their golden trumpets and
rise up in a host
of heavenly indifference.

DEMAIN (TOMORROW)

After Folon

Surely trees are reaching for some voice
The winter burglarized.
While they were sleeping

Luxuriously in thick green
Featherbeds, the wind slid
Into their arms, kissed them until they

Were shaken,
Dark bones clawing for the stars
Who speak a language of farewells.

Strip anything
And there's an agony of form
Contorting,

Desperate to acquire
What only camouflage can proffer
Or, failing that, resist.

If trees do nothing but foreshadow,
If they persist
Like war-cripples waving deformed stumps

At the windows of the comfortable,
If they hail a black planet in the dawn sky–
If it hurts to look at this,

Don't look;
Only keep thinking
One day ahead of yourself.

Apparitions of Earth

Even if you think the earth is hollow,
There is no sure way of getting into it
Except by tunneling through solid rock
Or exploring a deep cave
That may have no outlet.

Even if you think the earth is flat,
There is no way to prove it.
All evidence denies your theory
Of monsters lurking just off the edge of the map.

In your dream everything might be
The way you want it.
But if you wake thinking the earth is hostile,
You're still its child,
Its battered baby.
No court you can imagine
Will hold it responsible
For your bruises, fractures,
Your fatal concussion.

Even if the earth had a door,
It would not open
To the cavern of jewels guarded by evil dwarfs
Where the lamp in your hand would provide
Safe passage. Even if that door
Existed, it would not wear a sign
Saying *Walk Right In*
Like a store with a homely bell
Summoning the proprietor from behind
Chintz curtains.

Even if the earth were my body,
I could not house you
Or provision you against a future
Full of want.

SUMMER MEADOW IN GOTLAND

After Oskar Bergman

The flowers in this painting
Are all being pushed in one direction
By some malevolent presence. Their mouths open
In a vast yellow scream.
Massing the meadow like peasants
Driven from their huts with cudgels, they seem
Bewildered. No one has told them anything.

Revolution is born of such confusion,
Instructed not by minds like these
But by the grey breath that beats
Stem and stalk north by northeast.

The shambling army of yellowness
Looks to the sun. They bend their knees,
Pull forelocks of petals. Now it has begun.
Even the willows in the distance
Fly their green flags, advancing
Without ever glancing back to whatever
Set it all in motion.

How I Came to Write This Poem

First, set pieces
Clever as zircons,
Then weather,
A sky of cawing birds
And roiling clouds, my
Metaphor of badlands
Deceivingly pink and gold in dawn-light.

It is the angle of sun
Which captivates,
The molten canyon driving west
At sunset. The pearly morning
Centered with a redbird
Uttering his distinctive query
From the low bush beyond the south window.

The rimrocks hovering like
Ogre nursemaids,
Massive, flat-topped,
While the town below darkens
And sparkles.
A leaf is an anthem.
Everything stands for something.
We paddle still waters,
Making a silver groove
From which our existence,
Like waterbirds, perpetually slides forward.

A ring of firs. Black rock.
And always
The dream of white-eyed horses.

When you died, the voices chorused
Like migrating redwings
Filling the bare March trees
With amazing noise, then silence.

I could not open your book,
Examine the photograph, or look
At the slanted signature
Of your love. I could not
Feel.

Poetry repulsed me,
Its bleeding scab. Streaking windows
Of rain. Gravel embedded
In mud slick. Why
Write or sing or draw or think?
As Auden said, it changes
Nothing.

Last spring the rivers rose
Out of their banks in a hundred-year flood.
A terrified boy was swept away
As the news cameras followed. Men
Lowered ropes, attempting to grasp
An extremity as he boiled past
In the deluge, crying out.

This boy, a stranger, breaks
My heart. I wept for him
As I never could for you or for myself.
Today, the poem says
it will be spoken the way buds clench
Then burst in the false precursor flower.

The true leaf unfurls its nature,
Its delicate ribs, its fabric tough
And strange, green-skinned,
Thin-skinned, willing to suffer
Loss with the wind. All over earth,
Turning to powder, the least of us
Essential and here and now.

A WOMAN SCORNED

A woman scorned sets fire to the tent
Where the new wife is celebrating.
Carves her name and yours into a tree
Then chops that tree down with her nail file.
Cages a bird and teaches it to speak
In a language where every verb is an obscenity.
Combs her hair with broken glass until
It glitters like a million diamonds
That you stroke until your hands bleed rubies.
Watches how you sit quietly near the water
While she poisons the tea she is about to serve.
Drives a team of black horses down the avenue
Of your lovers, whipping them white as judges.
Climbs through the window that you forgot to secure
Wearing a burglar suit sewn of her eyelashes.
Picks a bouquet of jimsonweed, hydrangea,
Lily of the valley, poison ivy, rhododendron
To prove the base and beautiful can both be lethal.
Paints graffiti on the wall of your Facebook
And for good measure stamps a letter with your heart's-blood.
Enters your dream unbidden
Wearing the scarlet dress you once admired.
Paces up and down, up and down
Before your place of business.
Removes all the signposts pointing to
The street you used to live on when you were happy.

INCANTATIONS

Twisted forest light compels
An utterance of druids
Blue as agony.

A magpie reveres
Its treasures–
Tinfoil, a copper coin.

Think of the brigandage
Of crows. Crazed speech
That etches glass.

How priests
Raise chalices full of
Dead language.

Women whisper behind
Onyx rings. They want to tell
Unspeakable things.

The cant of politicians
Paints the wall with duplicity
Cowering like a cat the boys have stoned.

Sweet ejaculations quench
Years of burning. Come close. I'll
Show you what a spell is.

BEACHED BOATS

Waiting rooms.
Patients shifting on plastic chairs.
Nothing to look at but old magazines
And a painting of a gull-colored boat with an echo
Of scavenge, its paint flaking

Though you could imagine how once
Its spanking white prow parted waves.
Too elegant an image, perhaps,
For a rowboat of the sort
That came with rental cottages,
One with a knack for leaks, a bail can
Beneath the seat boards,

Lacking oarlocks and oars,
Hauled up on the bank
Of a perfectly calm pond whose far shore
Sports a motif of birch and fir.
A static composition, each blade
Of grass, tree trunk, or cast shadow

Exactly where you would expect it.
Patience. Compliance. Submission.
The brush strokes that shaped it
Never veered from the elegiac,
Never intimated any future beyond this one.

SUBJECTS

After Wislawa Szymborska

No more poems
Are to be written about spring.
Ordinary subjects are blessed:
Inkwells or eggs. An emerald ring.

Only the most adroit shall tackle
The large abstractions:
Truth, beauty, justice.

So we turn to the visible:
A fingernail in which a sun rises
Or sets in a cuticle of flesh.

A faded towel hanging from a rack,
Disconsolate as an abbess
Accused of sorcery.

A question mark's
Hook and eye
That will never catch

Or ever achieve the perfection
Of an answer that can't
Be questioned.

Seize river stones that, drying,
Have lost all luster.
Remember how they glistened
As the waters lapped, and find
The words to bring that back.

AUNT AGNES

Bedridden, beneath blankets,
Her leg black to the thigh.

The caregiver must have known.
It came out later, she was stealing.
But Mother also knew, I believe.
What could she have been thinking–
That the will of God must be endured?
Such speculation is useless,
And I'm not immune. I should have checked
On my weekly visit. She always said
"I'm fine. It's good to see you."

The surgeon says
Amputation is the only course.
"Agnes, do you want to live?" he asks.
What do you imagine she would say–
"Of course."

The surgery is not a success
Since there is no circulation
In the femoral artery. I sit
Beside the bed that vibrates–
To relieve pain, I guess. She smiles
And seems to rest.

The family doctor, who was away,
Returns with a frown dark as perdition.
"Who authorized this?"
His mouth tightens.

"We'll stop the antibiotic, let her
Die in peace." I'm not the one
To make that legal decision. Mother does. A sly
Something in her eyes. Maybe she knows best.

I remember how I dragged the barn cat
From behind the water tank where she went to die
One frozen winter morning,
Just prolonged her agony as I pestered
Her with penicillin injections. Feline
Leukemia took her anyway.
Like a hawk soaring with the power
Of thought, my principle was
Will is paramount. My daughter once said
"You think you can argue anyone into
Anything." And, yes, I did. I
Thought that.

Agnes dies easily. Mother weeps
And has a drink. Southern Comfort
Has become a resource. The hospital
Loses Agnes' leg; it can't be buried
In sanctified ground with the rest of her,
And this grieves Mother more than anything.

THE WINNERS

We are seated at a table
With the Super Ball winners,
A couple in their sixties
Who are 300 million-odd dollars
Richer than we are.

He was a plumber or electrician,
Some sort of tradesman, she
A housewife with bad teeth.

They frequented a local bar.
The tickets were bought by someone else
To whom they promised a million dollars.
When it turned out they had the numbers,

They reneged. A lawsuit was settled
Out of court. It was in the papers.

Of course, we don't bring that up,
Just listen while he expounds
On their world travels, flashing a
Pinky ring with a diamond
Like a trapdoor. She's bejeweled
As well and has new teeth
Regular as a picket fence.

They live in a new house
In a gated community
Where none of their old friends
Can get at them.

FINDERS

Hundreds of callers told him
He was an idiot not to keep
The bag of money he found while
Picking broccoli in his garden.

He'd thought of it, he said,
Conferred with his aged father.
Jobless, house gone to foreclosure,
He could have used it.

He called the sheriff instead.
The papers spread the story.
An honest man. If Diogenes
Had found him, he would have a halo

Made of lantern shine.
He unplugs the phone, ignores the doorbell.
Whoever left it might come back,
The plot of many a B-movie.

If no one ever claims it,
He'll have the right.
And if there is such a thing as justice,
He intends to get some teeth.

Up North

The door to his truck is hanging open,
So we know he came home drunk.
The husky raises an alarm
To rouse him, shirtless, hungover,
But glad to see us.

The cabin, a barrel stove, a cot,
Table and a chair. He puts a
Pot of coffee on. We sit outdoors
Waiting for the day to warm.

The outhouse is spic and span
As you might expect. A two-holer,
Calendar on a tack.

We go for a boat ride, 250 horse
Churning the waters of Devil Track,
The husky in the prow, blue-eyed and alert.
This lake allows for speed. That's what he likes.

His dad drowned in Superior
When a storm blew up and overturned
The canoe. Canoes are all you can use
Farther up in the BWCA.

"Those Sierra Clubbers outlawed
What a man needs. The snow machines.
Made it a no-flyover." His big hand slams
The wheel with disgust. "Granola eaters."

The sun is high, the sky a blue
I would describe as sapphire. It lifts his mood.
He's happy. Once he's got his deer,
He can skid logs all winter,
Enough for beer and a woman
When he wants one.

His brother, down to the Twin Cities,
Working in a factory, "That's what comes
Of getting a wife."
He shakes his head. "Time for a cold one."

Now we're headed up the trail.
He waves goodbye from the log bench.
The husky watches as we drive off
To see how the fires last year
Turned the forest ghostly.

SOUTHERN GOTHIC

Fueled with sippin' whiskey
Or in the yard with chickens,
The yarners float
Into mindsets of wisteria,
Imbecile narration, or the ghosts
Of one-legged women. Ancient crones
Tell the histories of subversion.

Once, hunting the pine brakes
Or collecting peahens, they spoke
A common tongue. My friend explains
The coon hunt– how the men gather
Around a fire with moonshine
To listen to hounds in the distance,

Their excited baying betraying
The kill– and those
Over-sweet stories
Intervals of docility where everything
That rises must converge.

REDHEADS

"Auburn," my mother said.
Rust is more like it.
Or chestnut like the mares
I always fell for
Despite the adage
Chestnut mare, Beware,
The one who almost killed me
Flipping at the oxer.

Old photographs: A stubborn Scotch-Irish
Grandmother, her copper bun
Pulled tight as temper. A hard life.
Her man shot dead, six kids to rear.

And there I am in pigtails, freckles,
Astride a sorrel called Rogue.
Or spring break in a bikini,
Flowing hair and fake ID,
Ready to get a scoop like Brenda Starr.

Now, a granddaughter, 12 years old,
Red hair waist-long. The same
Mutinous look I recognize
As I whip her again at Scrabble,
Then pacify with "Just a game,"
Which she smells out as insincere.
Shaking her garnet wealth
Star-strewn as Brenda's–
Who she's never heard of.
"I like to win," she says.
I know. That uncompromising
Stare. The spark in tinder.

Books

The argument against his authority
Was the absence of books
In his house in Avon.

Surely, those who love the word
Would treasure it between the spines
Of imagination.

The illuminated manuscripts
Slaved over by Irish monks
Still shine with gold leaf

And the hierarchical design
Of angels. Alexandria's great
Library bright with flame.

The conflagrations of Berlin.
Burghers flinging volumes
On the pyre.

The Critique of Pure Reason catches
Fire. *The Magic Mountain*
Erupts in pyrotechnics.

Meanwhile, in the quiet house,
Books caucus like citizens,
Shoulder to shoulder,

Like priests at their matins.
The importunate prayers.
How the world of definition

Resides in flimsy pages,
Binding you to the text,
To the common fonts.

Cyclist on Barr Road

The cyclist's T-shirt proclaims
Scintillating Language, which might be
The name of a rock band or the anthem
Of a Methodist youth group or the theme
Of the literary magazine at his junior college.
But I prefer to think he chose it
Independently the way he rides hunched over
Along the country road's verge, pedaling
Determinedly into the headwinds.

The language he propels on this second
Day of April, with the trees leafing
And the lilacs in early bloom and the
Squashed red debris of the maples under
His turning wheels, is one we can't predict.
But he seems to know where he is going,
Helmet-less, his burly calves muscling
For the coming rise as he rises to
Get up speed, crest, and disappear.

KINDERGARTEN—CHERNOBYL

Hundreds of child-sized gas masks,
So they always feared the
Meltdown. Living in the maw
Of power. The huge chimneys,
Their white plumes saluting
The dinge of sky. Now it's all
Wordless blackboards in an empty
Room where a headless doll becomes
The icon of those destined
To evacuate at the wheel of a toy car,
A small blue wreck
With a painted drum dropped
On its hood when someone fled
Or fell. The photos moldering
On the walls show the children
Earnestly performing calisthenics.
Ghost of a stuffed rabbit and now,
Years later, the animals return.
Wolves, wild boars, herds of feral
Horses. The little varmints
From the storybooks
That litter the forest floor
In a half-life. The teacher's final note:
Our nature walk has been cancelled.

FORECLOSURE

When everything was lost,
He snuck into the house
That once was his, pulled out
The copper pipes the color of
Her hair when they first met,
Removed the brass faucets,
Then the sink and the commode,
Sledgehammering them into
Oblivion the way she'd slept
In the arms of Luminol, ignoring his old
Rant. He tore out the cabinets,
Defaced the walls with sprayed
Obscenities that she'd laughed off,
Not caring one damn thing
How he felt, pulled up the carpets,
Poured grease on the wood floors.
She'd stripped memories
Like wallpaper, turned her head
Against the scrape of his whiskers.
He broke the bed into kindling.
She'd never sleep with any man
But him if he could help it. Then
He poured concrete down all the drains.
Try to fix that.

DEAR GHOSTS

Riding red horses,
War bridles, Mexican rowels,
Hills rolling in sage like blessings,
Thunderheads to the south.

Muzzle quilled like Saint Sebastian.
Jackrabbits soaring through
Decades of sleep. Rimrocks
Foreboding to the north. Stars

Stars, stars. Come into my dream,
You lost people I loved, saddled
With a darkness that traps you
Beneath inscribed stones.

In the unwoken world,
Elders believed you would
Ooze up gauzy as memory,
Speaking the glossolalia of scripture.

Speak to me, stunned in a white bed
Of perdition and misadventure.

SWALLOW

Soaring at dusk to feed on the wing,
Forked tail like a serpent's tongue,
Every year returning
To the steep loft. Harbinger
Of a thousand summers

When, lounging with tall
Frosted glasses of iced
Sweetness, we swallowed,
Grateful for the company of friends

Or in a lonesome bar knocking back
Shots of Jack Daniels,
Swallowing the hard words
Left unuttered.

That reflex was the last to fail.
You refused the tube while
You could still speak

Despite saliva, thick and sticky
Enough to glue wattled nests
To cobwebbed rafters
Of a dim, unforsaken

Sanctuary where your last breath
Coalesced to a lump of sorrow
In our throats, unable to swallow this.

EXACTLY

The horses proceed down the river path.
There is a place to ford.
The waters low enough.
The willows overhanging.

A vast hotel on the far bank
Full of mercenaries and warlords
Speaking languages we've never heard,
A rasp of brutal xylophones.

You can no more drown in this river
Than you can flounce into the drawing room
Where the dictator is drinking
Sour wine with his retinue.

That poems could be their legacy,
Not in a journal she wouldn't
Recognize, but in newspapers
That chronicled their escapades.

More ballad, though she knew little
Of such distinctions, imagining gunfire,
Robbery, wrecked cars, fire, disfigurement
Could be absolved with the cliché

Of doomed lovers– Romeo and Juliet,
Tristan and Isolde, Heloise and Abelard–
Unlikely emblems in those
Dreary east-Texas towns.

Newsboys shouted their latest
Exploits to readers sick of the black
Slag of depression. Her nervy paeans,
Jejune, almost touching, preserved

For years after their riddled bodies
Were laid out for exposition: a coda
To her rhymed renditions of
How they would go down.

THE SKETCH ARTIST

Slash of charcoal– a mustache.
Frown lines. A profile sharply drawn
All black-on-white the way a body

Might crumple in a porcelain tub,
A fall from grace in an oddly dry
Basin. The defense's story.

Barrage of small creases penciled
Around the eyes. Cold as bullets
Or the sleeper hold cops master.

Exhumed, the skull seems bashed.
Quick outline: the prosecutor's
Finger pointing. Or perhaps

The natural resolution of decay.
The hearsay sisters, mouths crosshatched
With anger. Return to that

Immovable stare. Quirk of lip
Sarcastic or snarling or just about
To grin. That charm, that lure

Flashing just below the surface
Where another woman lazily swims,
Liking what she sees here.

HOODIES

Menacing as a monk
At the Inquisition,
The secular arm extended
With a torch to light
The faggots beneath the feet
Of the unabsolved.

The peasant uprising,
Red hoods and pitchforks,
Advancing on the palace
Of improprieties, their cadenced
Slogans and blunt faces
Dark with resolution.

Slinking midnight avenues
In twos or threes,
Hunched, stony
With intent.
Settling next to you,
Dozing fitfully,
In the last subway car
On its final run.

SANDALS

This side of the border, they discard
All that weighs them down:
Empty water bottles,
A pastiche of plastic,
Fake IDs, addresses
Of cousins in LA or Chicago,
If they can get that far
On blisters and sweat.

When the sun at noon scorches earth
Or the desert night lays a cold
Coverlet on shuddering flesh,
They squat in creosote bushes,
Patrols shining lights to stun them
Like animals.

Thousands have perished,
Some still sitting as if alive,
Staring sightless in exhaustion
And despair. Others
Baked sere, just bones clad in rags
Gnawed by javelina.

Four sandals
Filthy with the dust
Of pilgrimage,
His flanked by hers,
As if they wound
Their bodies together
Before stepping out and
Walking off to nowhere.

ARIA

Singing began as a way to capture
Evil spirits. Caught in the cage
Of the larynx to choke on ash
And harmony, desire fills their
Goatish pupils as if nightingales
Collaborated on a symphony
Or a Chopin mazurka danced
The gaudy excess from their
Bones. Maria Callas lifts her voice
From the ocean where sperm whales
Vocalize, where sirens call
From isolate rocks. Those spirits chained
To the mast begin to tremble, to
Evaporate like ghosts clamped
In a textbook, like a revision
Of Revelation– the pale horse
Whinnying, nodding his head in
Obligation, stamping a hoof
In one drumbeat. And now the aria
Begins to soar like a murder of angels
Or demons, like crows
Hoarse with ambition. Keep singing.
The bars. The grace notes.
The treble clef. The voice a cappella
To save us.

SILK POEM I

In a conversation chiseled out of silk,
We drink the milk of human kindness
Then spit it out. The clout of old convention
Reins us in like heavy horses. The watercourses
Run, the ancient mills turn and turn,
And it is time itself we burn, the maple leaves
Embarrassed, fallen red as refugees from heaven.
Six or seven years have passed. Remember how we met.
It was a Tuesday, wet, the sidewalks gleaming
As the lions before the institute stood dreaming
In their stone magnificence. Now we might wince
To think of how gingerly we kissed as the mist
Rose from the lake in gowns of women
Lost or drowned. This story goes around and around
Until the evidence is proved, the grave
Grooved in a prurience of desire that
Fulminates and lingers and expires.

SILK POEM II

Silkworms depend on mulberry leaves
The way you and I depend on trust.
Their weight increases ten-thousandfold
From hatching. Fattened as we become
With love, they spin silvery cocoons
By nodding their heads in agreement
Until they are liquid as we are with desire.
Miles later, we drive into a distance
Of sustainable comfort; the little car
Of our cohabitation encloses us
Like a silken casket. But no one is safe.
The farmers kill the sleeping larvae
With the sort of heat that inflames our bodies.
We had never thought about danger– how the fibers
That connect us could be unwound;
That a single thread could be what matters, so
Fragile any word could disrupt its continuity.

SILK POEM III

A woman wearing silk will not sift flour
In hell's kitchens. She will not let flowers
Wilt in the crystal vase. She keeps the secrets
Of the forbidden city
Of her body. Her bridal gown
Is of red silk and, when she speaks,
Silk threads spin into propositions.
What she wants
Is what you will learn to want.

In Islam men are banned from silks,
The sly womanly feel of such garments.
A man might step out of himself
Into an otherness that frightens him.
"Don't fear," she calls, in tones of black silk.
"You may touch the gown
Of your future, climb the silken ropes
To paradise." She throws
Scarf after scarf of colorful silks
Over his shoulders, his arms. He's
Drowning in silks, in slippery seas of them.

SILK POEM VII

Lei-Tzu invented silk 3,500 years
Before the birth of Christ, never imagining
How her reign on earth would be identified.
She might have scorned such western
Ideology. Only she herself and her descendants
Were worthy, were due the elegance
Of silks, the intricate weave of
Dynasty after dynasty. Sericulture
Of the select. A magpie inked on silk
In the 10th century. Saris
Of Bhoodan Pochampally, the silk city,
Interwoven with silver thread
Like rivers stippled onto maps
The way a bride is wedded to
Tradition. Muga, the golden silk of Assam.
At the second inauguration, the president's
Wife wears a coat of silk jacquard
Patterned like the expensive ties
Men of property sport. A poet reads
How "every language spoken into one wind"
Is a silken thread that binds us together
With tensile strength– bonds that resist
Breakage, that suture a wounded nation,
Let men drift from the sky under halos.
Think how Clyde Barrow yearned
For the silk shirt of the prosperous gangster,
A spell against the poverty
Of his imagination.

LINEN POEM

Let us testify to the integrity of linen.
The winnowing, retting and scutching,
How it is heckled with combs.
The mummy wraps of archeology
Retained in the sarcophagus
Of the unearthed tomb.
Leviticus proscribes against
Mingling linen and wool,
Abomination of animal and vegetable
Kingdoms. The purity of linen
Must never be questioned. Linen
Of good intentions, of the flaxen fields.

Linen Poem II

Observe the colonial
Diplomat in his linen suit
Strolling the boulevards,
Wiping his damp brow
With a linen handkerchief.
The irregular polygons
Coarse and cooling.
Watch the woman in a
Slubbed linen sheath
Lift her glass of G&T as she
Lounges in a lawn chair
Viewing a cricket match in the year
Before the Great War. Look up
Into the night sky as the moon rises.
There floating like stars are angels
Clad in fine white linen.

SYNTHETICS POEM—POLYESTER

In the photograph, he stands in
A sky-blue leisure suit,
Stacked heels, gold chain. He has
A beard. She is dressed in a plaid
Skirt, purple vest, a blouse with big
Sleeves. Her hair is long and ironed
Straight. Shag rug, slinky sheets
On the waterbed, everything
Chemical and irritating. They only
Wanted what everyone wanted.
She painted her eyelids blue.
He started wearing faux silk briefs.
That's how she knew.

SYNTHETICS POEM—NEOPRENE

Sleek and black as wet seals
Sprawled on rocks like intestines
Or bags overstuffed with something
Unclean. Otherworldly divers with
The bends or sucking air the way
Gypsies do scamming the housewives.
Fishermen in waders casting
Imposter flies as a woman
Puts on the face mask of desire,
The wet suit skin-tight
To expel the cold as she floats
Faceup in a radical emulsion,
Thinking all of this is simply
Chemistry.

WOOL POEM II

Pattern inherent in place.
Fingers ply the needles,
Cable, honeycomb, basket, diamond.
Knit and purl. Memory guides
Over moor and peat bog. Here's
Where a slipped stitch left a hole
Of falsehood. Undyed to clothe
The men of Aran. Flimsy currachs
Bound for the mainland. How
Wet wool fingers the drowned.

WOOL POEM IV

They wear those long johns
All winter. Imagine the stink,
How their wives must shudder.
The reek of barnyard, of sweat
Dried stiff as a stallion's cock.
The beard scraped to scratch the way
A union suit flays them rough beneath
Overalls and flannel. Let blizzards
Come, the wives fly off
The handle. They are ready.

WOOL POEM VII

Gather the nucleus of a poem
The way children heedlessly
Snatch wool from heather,
Stray bits like a litany
Repeating into oblivion.
Attention drifts in aimless
Tasks, not even mulling
But bagging what is given
By accident, how the sheep passed
Leaving tufts of impression
That suddenly weave into
Inevitable patterns.

LACE POEM

Erect an effigy of lace,
Fine-tuned as Mozart,
Correct as an equation
Of the lost world of distinctions.
Cutwork approximations beset
With interstices, how a dream
Of open spaces snares the heart.
Venetian gros point, the finest art
Of needlework embroidered with
Loops and picots. Crocheted lace of the poor
Imitations of civility. Lace of the
Bridal veil, vestments of the bishop,
Baptismal cap. Swirl of design
Handworked by women going blind.

LACE POEM II

Chantilly lace made with bobbins
Pinning threads to a pillow
Stuffed with oat straw,
Patterned with flowers.
Threads of black silk turned light and shadow
To intrigue, mantillas, shawls,
The mourning edges of a collar,
Gloves of a seductress.
Marie Antoinette loved such lace,
The precious separations
Ensnaring words she may never
Have said: cake or bread. Her
Little Papillon in the tumbril.
The lacemakers of Chantilly
Following her to the guillotine.

DOOMSDAY

Below ground, dystopia rules
A dark universe of cached
Foods, kerosene, and bottled water.
Ammunition for as many guns
As it takes to keep the neighbors out.

The child he took for company
Is wrong, won't look him in
The eye, play checkers, talk,
Just bobs his head this way
And that as if acknowledging
Some inner music.

Now they shout down the air
Pipe. He won't be misled,
Calculates how long he can
Hold out. Up above they lift
Voices to heaven. He's 65, the kid
Is maybe 7. He spreads the
Bread with jam, says "Here."

BACK IN EDEN

"Dogs are our link to paradise. They don't know evil or jealousy or discontent. To sit with a dog on a hillside on a glorious afternoon is to be back in Eden, where doing nothing was not boring—it was peace." —Facebook posting 2-2-2013

They were bored in Eden
Feasting on peaches, strawberries,
Grapes, and hyacinths. Anything
Was feasible and therefore boring.

She kept visiting the crooked tree
Where the snake coiled in its
Hermitage. He told her it was
Forbidden, this kind of knowledge.
He told her that their naked bodies
Were perfect, that if they just fucked more
They wouldn't be bored. But she

Had a different vision. Her mouth
Watered at the notion of apples, round,
Crimson, succulent. The snake said
Have a taste, and once she did she wanted
More and more– the whole vast world beyond
The gates. He let her feed him

Apples when she promised
Exotic sexual pleasures. Listen,
There were no dogs in Eden.
They were out there in the wilderness
And they were hungry.

MARCH 1ST WITH CROWS

A murder of crows embitters
The bleak afternoon.
Collective-noun preening
How they mob the hawks
Or cry harsh accolades
To an indifferent sky.

The symbolism of crows
Is specious– like shotgunning
The trees where they huddle,
Rewriting history in a
Script of ragged wings,
Dark angels of prescience. With
Knapsacks of torment, they
Fashion their nests in your mind.

Crows with their bullet eyes
And Dickensian smirks
Jammed with chanceries,
Lawsuits, crime.

BIRDBIRDISTHEWORD

Crouched in the paddies with the wounded
Waiting, hushed, until the hum
Like a loud dragonfly, the rotors whirring.
"Bird," they whispered. "Birdbirdistheword."

Named that colt for those lofty
Memories of rescue. A certain promise.
He could fly. Won the million-dollar
Delta Jackpot as a two-year-old. A Derby
Contender, maybe. Then he was wounded,

The way good ones too often are. Went on
To win a few. Retired to stud.
Lucky as the ones who made it home
With gimpy legs or confusions.

Died in a barn fire one year later.
So much for luck. So much
For that guy on the riverbank,
Mind whirling like the rotors lifting up.

Yak Culture

A documentary: the nomads of Tibet.
The Yak gives everything– milk, cheese,
The tent– they burn its dung, it carries
Their burdens, it carries them.

It seems a foolish, shaggy beast.
Square-headed with bangs, it looks truculent,
Jumps about awkwardly, runs off when it can,
Then is recaptured by the man on a thin white pony.

The woman wrestles oblongs of cheese,
Their winter provender. She says it is the woman
Who works. The man creams yellow ointment–
Perhaps made of cheese– onto his pimples.
He believes he would be handsome, if not
For these blemishes. They laugh, they tell
Yak jokes, the main topic of conversation:
The Yak, its offspring, its two-year-olds
Which are naughty, claims the man
In tones of affection. They have an infant.
It is fat, they say happily, so it may live,
Unlike the others.
The woman bows and chants. Her teeth are bad.
The man remembers all the women he slept with.
Now he loves this one. Together, they pull
The wool of Yaks into coils.

They travel to winter pasture, a colony of Yaks
Carrying all they need. I begin to envy
How they can know everything about their lives.
I think with longing of this simplicity.

They envy the neighbors' prayer flags,
Newer, more colorful, fluttering prettily.
The man mourns that he cannot read.
The woman hopes her daughter will be a nun–
An easier life, a life of prayer culture.

I want to say "Be content.
Be content with Yakness."
They smile, they sing of the joy of being Tibetan.
I believe they know I am watching,
That such conclusions exhaust me.
They milk the Yaks. The woman nurses
The child. Listen, your hour in this box is over,
And I have learned nothing,
Nothing that I can use.

THE CHILDREN

Sandy Hook Elementary School, Newtown, Connecticut

The children march,
Each with a hand on the shoulder
Of the one ahead. Streaming
To the playground. Their eyes
Closed against the others,
Riddled like broken ornaments
A week before the holiday.

To clasp the one before you
Is how to move through the world
In charity, how to hope the tinsel
Of error will not fall upon you,
A shivering glitter
Of terrible clarity.

THE BOATS

Mithridates survived 17 days before expiring.

Head, hands, and feet stuck out
Between two wooden boats.
The face, the extremities smeared
With honey for insects, stinging wasps,
Flies. Force-fed so that he lives
In the torment of worms and maggots
Eating him from the inside out. A death
Reserved for traitors.

A cordon drawn. He needs to hide.
They'd walked from the blast
Satisfied. Now it's gone wrong.
His brother's body beneath wheels.
Bleeding, he crawls under the tarp
Of a white boat in someone's yard.
All day, silent, trapped in torment
Eating him from the inside out.

RADIANCE

A vast swirling suffusion of red exploding
Into stars and planets rushing in an abundance
Of galaxies. Each sun a hot circle of radiation,
A fiery industry of gasses and flares.

7,000 rads. Shoved in the cylinder. Purple arrows
On the belly showing where the beam
Should incinerate the rogue cells. Risk vs. benefit.
The words of scientists or priests.

Marie Curie delved in potent rays,
How to deflesh the body to the bone, to exhibit
Each secret passageway. For this she atoned:
White armies in her veins, armed with flames.

Of those treated, 35 percent will suffer
Radiation enteritis. Scarred canyons blind and twisting,
Arroyos of inflammation, blockages, a tube forced
Down the nose to decompress ballooning arcades.

For years after the mushroom cloud, they kept on
Dying. Those who weren't instantly blasted
To stardust. So little was known. Even the feet of
Children thrust into machines to measure for shoes.

Women painted watch dials to glow in the dark,
Then glowed with the burning agony of saints.
It is true; we are products of comets, our atoms
Delivered with violence.

Solar flares that disrupt satellites.
The flare in the gut.
Gods of fire and sword.
The savage theology of the radiant way.

Acknowledgments

After Hours: "Subjects," "The Children"

Ann Arbor Review: "Exactly"

Ascent: "The Wyoming Pagoda"

Barrelhouse: "How I Came to Write This Poem"

Black Heart Magazine: "Synthetics Poem– Polyester," "Synthetics Poem– Neoprene"

Blue Bear Review: "Dear Ghosts"

Blue Unicorn: "Karen's Quilt Shop"

Boston Literary Magazine: "Doomsday"

Broad!: "Collected Poems of Bonnie Parker"

Broadkill Review: "Books," "Radiance"

Cat's Eye: "Mixed Marriage"

Dead Snakes: "The Winners," "Yak Culture"

Deimos Ezine: "Gargoyles"

Earth's Daughters: "Kindergarten– Chernobyl"

FutureCycle: "Sandals," "Swallow"

Gargoyle: "The Wingback Chair"

Kansas Quarterly: "Apparitions of Earth"

Local Gem Anthology: "Finders"

Main Street Rag: "A Fella Maybe"

Mid-American Review: "On Angels"

Milk Sugar: "Redheads"

Miller's Pond: "March 1st with Crows"

Misfit Magazine: "Back in Eden," "Hoodies," "Frankenstein"

The Pedestal: "Demain"

Pinyon: "A Woman Scorned"

Pirene's Fountain: "Incantations"

Plainsongs: "Aunt Agnes"

Poetry Quarterly: "Chains"

Prick of the Spindle: "Silk Poem II"

Slant: "Beached Boats"

Smartish Pace: "Summer Meadow in Gotland"

Spoon River Poetry Review: "Meditation of the Witch"

Stone Boat: "Foreclosure"

Storm Cellar: "What is Saved"

Thunder Sandwich: "Southern Gothic"

Turtle Island Quarterly: "Aria," "Linen Poem," "Linen Poem II"

Unicorn: "The Piano Student"

Wilderness House: "Up North"

Zest Literary Journal: "Wool Poem II," "Wool Poem IV,"
    "Wool Poem VII"

Cover design and illustration, "The Wingback Chair," by Ian King (tunnelsunstudios.com); author photo by Nancy Knott; interior book design by Diane Kistner (dkistner@futurecycle.org); Chaparral Pro with Copperplate titling

ABOUT FUTURECYCLE PRESS

FutureCycle Press is dedicated to publishing lasting English-language poetry books, chapbooks, and anthologies in both print-on-demand and ebook formats. Founded in 2007 by long-time independent editor/publishers and partners Diane Kistner and Robert S. King, the press incorporated as a nonprofit in 2012. A number of our editors are distinguished poets and writers in their own right, and we have been actively involved in the small press movement going back to the early seventies.

The FutureCycle Poetry Book Prize and honorarium is awarded annually for the best full-length volume of poetry we publish in a calendar year. Introduced in 2013, our Good Works projects are anthologies devoted to issues of universal significance, with all proceeds donated to a related worthy cause. Our Selected Poems series highlights contemporary poets with a substantial body of work to their credit; with this series we strive to resurrect work that has had limited distribution and is now out of print.

We are dedicated to giving all of the authors we publish the care their work deserves, making our catalog of titles the most diverse and distinguished it can be, and paying forward any earnings to fund more great books.

We've learned a few things about independent publishing over the years. We've also evolved a unique, resilient publishing model that allows us to focus mainly on vetting and preserving for posterity the most books of exceptional quality without becoming overwhelmed with bookkeeping and mailing, fundraising activities, or taxing editorial and production "bubbles." To find out more about what we are doing, come see us at www.futurecycle.org.